Compute in Comfort

"The aim of this book is to give you the tools needed to guide you in your quest towards feeling better while working on a computer"

Kimberly Cox
with Andrea Hughes

This book is dedicated to our family and friends.

About the Author

Kim Cox was born in Biloxi, Mississippi in 1966 and has worked in the physical therapy field for over 20 years. In 1998 she graduated from Florida State University with a B.S. in Exercise Physiology. She received a California license for PTA in 1993.

For the past 8 years, Kim has specialized in Ergonomics in the workplace. She has worked with many companies in San Diego and individuals. Kim has certifications as a Job Site Analysis Evaluator and Advanced Ergonomics for Office Workstations. Kim also received certification as a Certified Ergonomic Assessment Specialist I and II (CEAS I, CEASII). She also develops Exercise Programs.

Kim believes that good
ergonomic designs help the
productivity of employees, and
are pivotal for company
efficiency and long -term
profitability. Intervention targets
a happier, healthier workplace
that is more productive, safer,
and certainly less costly.

Table of Contents

INTRODUCTION

Why posture is important….
a lot of people injure their back.

Twenty percent of injuries seem
to be caused by work design and
with better set ups and equipment
we can work to fix that. But, it's
not a large percentage. Where is
the other 80% coming from?
What is the big problem here???
US!! We have bad habits. We are
de-conditioned and have poor
flexibility. How many of you are
doing a regular exercise
regimen? Who does cartwheels
when they get home from work?
At home do you squat to pick up
things, such as toys, shoes, etc.?
When you need something above
your desk, do you stand up ?
Hmmm....

Chapter 1

The Spine

Here is a model of the spine, our back bone, the instrument that allows us to walk upright, stand tall, and to cry out in pain if it suffers any kind of problem or injury! The spine is made up of seven , cervical vertebrae, 12 thoracic vertebrae, five lumbar vertebrae, and the sacrum. See the natural curves throughout? Those curves need to be your focus.

The Vertebrae

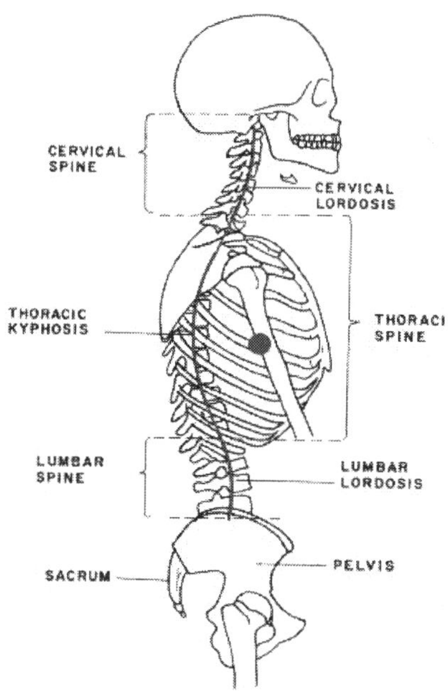

The interlocking design of the vertebrae allows it to move in segments. Between the bones that make up the vertebrae, there are pads called discs. Each disc is a circular pad filled with a gelatin type substance that is under constant pressure—especially from your movements. The disc acts like a shock absorber between the vertebrae and allows for a smooth segmental movement when you move. I like to call it the "jelly donut" because this is what it resembles. It has a thick casing, and a thick gooey filling like a jelly donut. If you or someone you know has been told they have arthritis, degenerative joint disease, or a narrowing of the joint spaces in the spine— it's because the discs have been compressed over time and have lost some or all of their fluid. Try bending and extending; can you feel the compression on the back part of your disc and a stretch in other places? When you bend over at the computer, the same thing happens—just from sitting. This is why therapists (and your mother) are always telling you to maintain your curve in your back and keep your back straight— sitting, standing, squatting, reaching—it doesn't matter—

keep your back straight!
However, we need to look again
at the curves in your spine to
understand what true correct
posture means. Let's look at
your low back curve (lumbar
curve). There should be a slight
curve inward toward your belly.
Then, it starts to slightly curve
back away from your belly. And,
lastly, the spine will curve
inward again toward your throat.
The key to good and proper
posture is to maintain those
curves at all times. This is
because when the spine is in the
"S" curve, then all the pressures
placed on the discs are evenly
dispersed and the muscles of the
back and neck work
synergistically with no stress on
them. If you don't work towards
achieving this position,
eventually, the wear and tear on
your disc will become more and

more of an issue and the joint spaces will begin to approximate or touch one another. The result …..wear and tear on the joint surfaces which could result in such common injuries as a herniated disc, carpel tunnel syndrome or sciatica pain—to name a few.

When the disc becomes really irritated and inflamed, it will begin to bulge and swell. This, in turn, puts pressure on the nerve roots between the vertebrae and possibly on the spinal cord. When you hear someone say they have a slipped disc, their disc hasn't really slipped. What it has done is swelled and bulged and finally herniated and possibly ruptured. Thankfully, most back injuries never reach this stage and are usually only a muscle, tendon, or ligament sprain.

Uncomfortable? Yes, but also treatable!

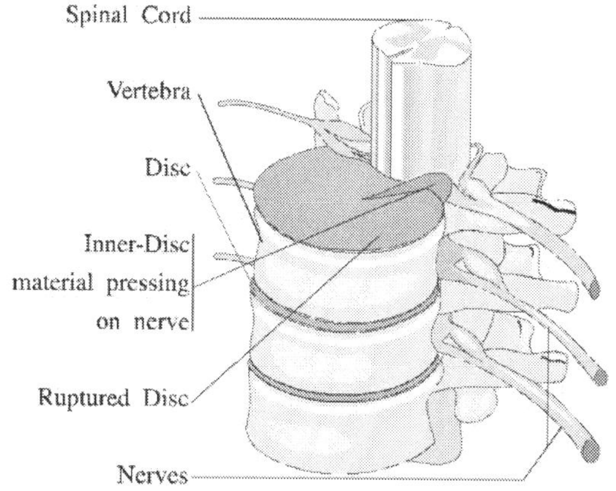

No pain, no gain does not apply here. Any time you feel pain, listen to it. Pain is a message from your body saying enough is enough. Often people will say it's just a twinge.
Well you usually feel a twinge when you have a small tearing of the ligaments' deep structures. And, guess what, if you ignore these little twinges the pain and the injury will only get worse. The body as a machine is smart enough to try and protect itself.

Any time you feel stiff is the body's attempt to repair injury by inducing inflammation and decreasing mobility. The inflammation settles in and causes tissue irritation, which, in turn, registers as discomfort. So, the motto should be "no pain, no pain".

One of the most common causes of back injuries is lifting incorrectly. However, just sitting incorrectly, be it at a computer, driving, or watching television can also cause a back injury. Also a number of other injuries can occur when sitting incorrectly at a computer.

The importance of a neutral spine —which means having the "S" curve at all times—must be reinforced. This maintains disc alignment and the stresses on the other structures. Keep the jelly donut pressure evenly distributed!

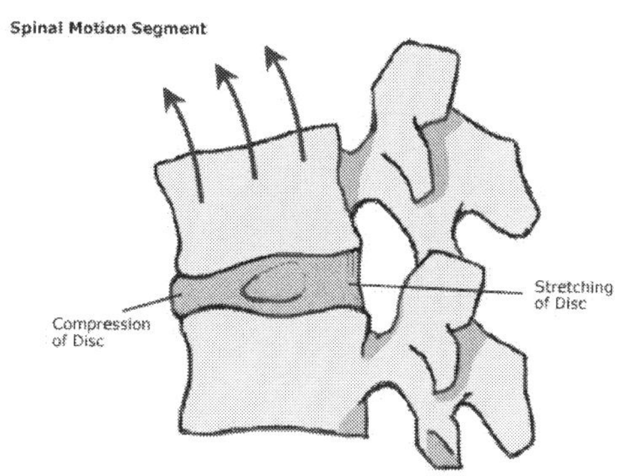

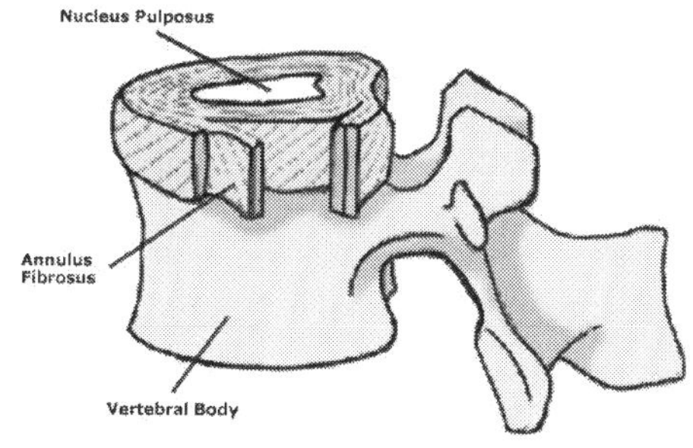

Think about your movements throughout the day. Something as simple and frequently done throughout the day as bending over to get something out of a drawer can cause an injury. For example, when you are sitting in your chair at your desk and lean over to open a file drawer, you are twisting in the flexed position or winding up your spine. In this position, compressive forces in the discs along with the stretching that occurs on the other structures are extremely dangerous. You need to look at your work station and assess how you can reduce or eliminate the need to twist during your day.

Throughout the day we get caught up in what we are doing and don't pay attention to what our body is doing. You feel a twinge, you ignore it, too busy to stop, have to get this done. We all do it!! And then….one day you wake up and cannot move….crying like a baby and swearing that you don't know what you've done. Well I do! **YOU DIDN'T PAY ATTENTION TO YOUR BODY.**
If you don't want an injury, start listening to your body and pay attention to your body positions. Once you are aware of the correct body position— and have trained your body to be in that position—you'll greatly reduce your likelihood of becoming injured. **Remember ….You are not the only one that has to live with the pain of an injury.**

Your loved ones don't want to
have to take care of you or listen
to you whining about how much
it hurts.
Do everyone a favor and…..slow
down and listen to your body!

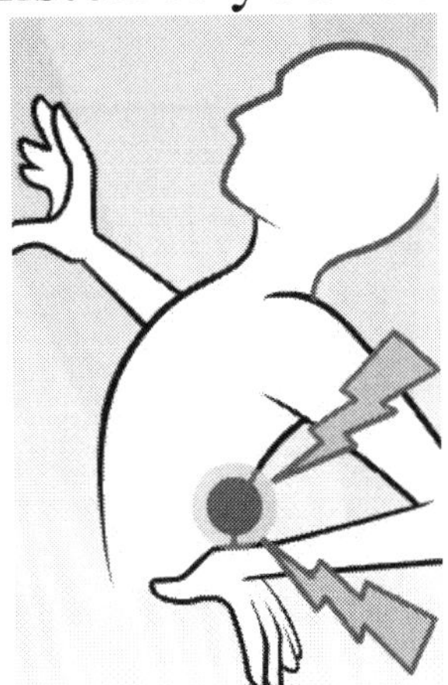

As noted before, the wear and
tear of the discs and
surrounding tissues lead to injury
over time. With increased
abdominal mass the wear and
tear is accentuated.
**—yes there are many thin
people with injured backs!**

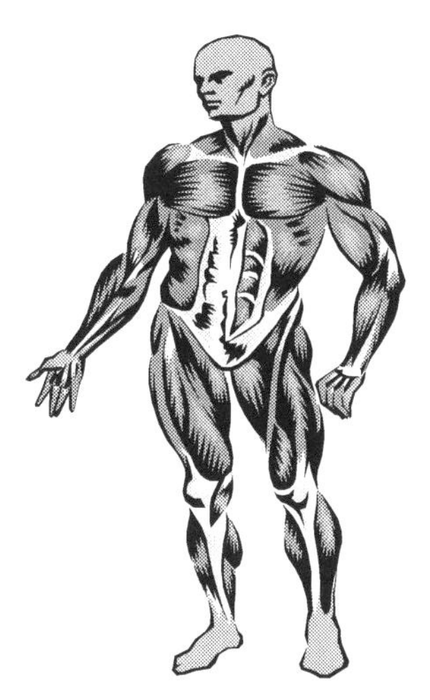

So, if you don't have washboard abdominal muscles, and even if you do, using correct body mechanics, i.e. maintaining the curves in your spine, working smart, knowing your lifting limits, changing your workstation to fit you, and ultimately staying strong and flexible will help you avoid injury.

Chapter 2

Correct Sitting Posture

The number of people walking around and sitting with poor posture could be called an epidemic. And, the only way to get rid of this epidemic is by educating people to pay more attention to their posture—the first step in having them develop good posture.

Your brain does not know correct from incorrect posture—**it only knows what it is used to.** Hence, this is why it feels so awkward to change any habit.

"If you keep on doing what you've always done, you'll keep on getting what you have always gotten." (Michael Clouse) In terms of poor posture, this means pain, tiredness and stiffness.

The key to good posture is in the alignment of the pelvis when sitting. Unfortunately, most chairs don't allow you to align your pelvis correctly and encourage slumping. Slumping in your seat may feel relaxing, but it is only shifting strain from one part of your body to another and anytime there is strain on any part of your body you increase your chances of getting an injury.

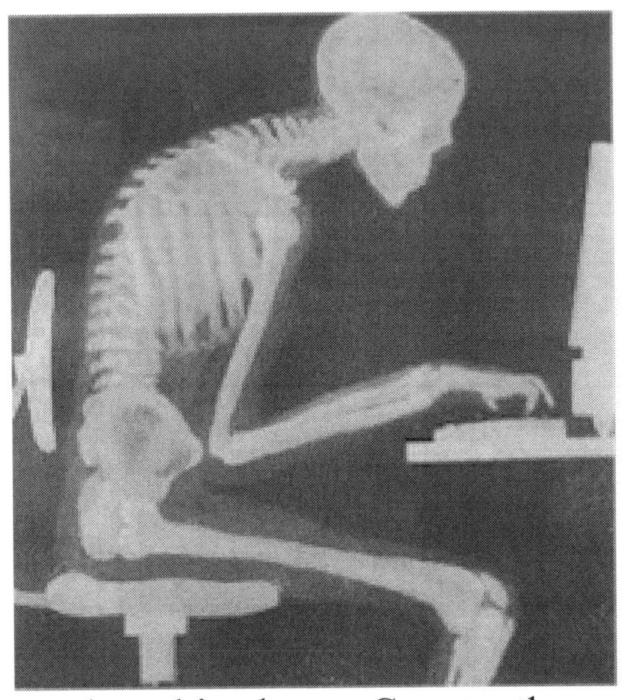

Look at this photo. Constantly bending forward while sitting at your desk and not maintaining a neutral spine will eventually cause permanent bone structure changes. **And, you thought osteoporosis was your only concern!**

 A neutral spine is not stiff and ramrod straight. Rather, it is gently curved but not slouching over. To achieve a neutral spine, sit with an equal amount of weight on the bones of each buttock and push your buttocks, back, and shoulders against the back of the chair. By doing this and having both feet flat on the floor your spine should naturally curve and go into a neutral position. If your chair doesn't have a built-in contour for the base of your back, simply put a small pillow or a rolled towel there. This will provide a gentle curve at the base of your back and help you to maintain the correct posture while sitting. Another thing many people don't think about is that something as simple as having a wallet or phone in your back pocket can cause your posture to be misaligned. **So…empty your back pockets!**

One more thing…whether you're sitting or standing—on average—most people should not stay in the same position for more than 15 or 20 minutes before moving.

How to Keep a Correct Sitting Posture

1. Distribute your weight evenly on the bones of each buttock.
2. Ensure that your chair's height enables you to place both feet flat on the floor, if unable, then use a footrest.
3. Use a rolled towel, small pillow, or lumbar pad if your chair is not built to support the natural curve of your lower back to achieve a hip to torso angle of 90 degrees to 105 degree angle.

4. Ensure your thighs are parallel to the floor.
5. Ensure your knees and hips form a 90 degree to 105 degree angle when your feet are flat on the floor
6. Ensure that your chair's armrests do not stop you from gently relaxing your shoulders when you are keyboarding

CORRECT POSTURE

Chapter 3

Awareness

Many times throughout the day we all do things and we don't give a second thought to the strain we are putting our body through. Here are some of the activities we all do without a second thought to the unnecessary physical stress on our bodies.

- Cradling a telephone between our head and shoulder
- Sitting in one position for extended periods
- Crossing your legs while sitting
- Reaching for improperly placed equipment

- Twisting to view a monitor that is off center
- Sitting and looking at the computer with your chin forward

The following photos are examples of what you should not be doing!

Chapter 4

Tips for the day

Getting a leg up…
Computer workers frequently shift into awkward positions, such as sitting on one leg, in an attempt to get more comfortable. This posture can impede circulation and make you lethargic. If you find yourself doing this because you don't have adequate foot support, try lowering your chair or adding a footrest. If it's just a habit, try to break it. Improved circulation will improve your comfort and energy throughout the day.

Don't shrug off good posture…
Occasionally shrugging your
shoulders during computer work
can help stretch muscles and
increase blood flow. However,
keeping your shoulders hunched
on a regular basis can result in
pain or injury. This occurs if the
keyboard is too high, the chair
too low, or if the chair arms push
up on the elbows. Relaxing your
shoulders and keeping your
elbows close to your side helps
shrug off pain and possible
injury.

Don't stick your neck out…
Taking risks is common in
business. But don't do it with
your posture. Craning your neck
forward during computer use
increases risk of neck injury. If
you have difficulty seeing the
monitor, move it closer, increase
font size, or have your vision
checked. If you lean forward in
your chair out of habit, form a
new habit. Sit back. Keep your
head over your shoulders and
your neck out of pain.

Office hypnosis…

Eye muscles—just like other muscles—get tired when held in a static posture. Staring at a monitor at a fixed distance forces your eye muscles to work hard to converge the image while focusing on the screen. To eliminate static vision and periodically give your eyes a rest focus away from the screen every 20 minutes on an object 20 feet and read something for 20 seconds (20-20-20 rule) to help prevent eyestrain.

Don't be so edgy

You may find yourself on the edge of your seat during a horror movie. But remember, sitting on the edge of your chair while working on the computer places strain on back muscles and ligaments. Try to sit all the way back each time. If necessary, move your monitor closer or make the characters larger for easy viewing. Let the chair do its work of supporting your back so you can do your work more comfortably.

Keep it Moving

Sitting still may be proper demeanor for schoolchildren but it is inadvisable for computer workers. A fixed posture held for too long can reduce blood flow to muscles and increase fatigue. Over time it can lead to pain and injury. Remember, regular movement keeps muscles from getting stiff and sore. So readjust your chair often, stretch regularly, and vary your tasks throughout the day.

Our bodies compensate and are able to put up with bad habits for a very long time, then, one day, BAM! You have an injury. You know what I mean, the guy that bends over to pick up a pencil, throws his back out. It wasn't from that one act; it's from years of poor posture, or just being out of shape.

You must learn to feel when your body is misaligned. Is your head forward? Is your pelvis collapsed? Are you slouching your shoulders? The key is being aware and correcting it.

Correcting yourself over and over will re-train the brain, and automatically correctly align itself.

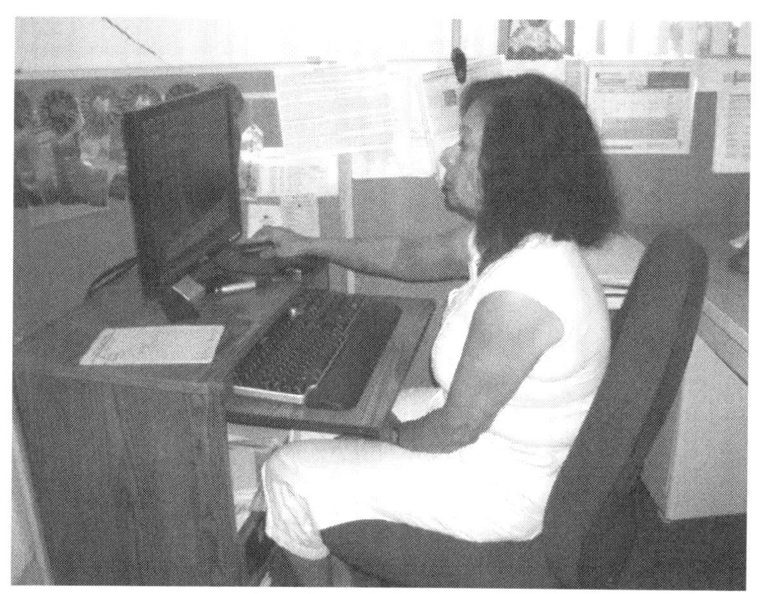

Before

After

Chapter 5

Why Stretching?

Muscles need stretching throughout the day to get blood flow to them so they continue to work properly. The tendency of human nature is to ignore signs and symptoms that our body is giving us. "Oh, that twinge will go away soon. I must finish this project by 5:00." The problem with ignoring these signals is that you are ignoring the body's message telling you to take a break and get some more oxygen to that area and flush out the toxins.

The repetitive motions we have to do in a day cause the small muscles to fatigue. Have you ever sat too long only to find when you get up you're stiff? That's from non- movement of muscles and tendons!! It's along the same lines as lactic-acid build up because the chemicals are stationary in the muscles and joints and cause a sensation of stiffness. Therefore, the best way to keep things moving and healthy is to stretch for at least a minute every hour throughout the day.

Here are some reasons you should always stretch.

- Stretching allows blood flow to the small muscle groups that are overused when typing and mousing. Blood is brought to the areas to bring oxygen and to remove the toxins and chemicals that pool there from static motions.
- Studies show that high repetitive movements require more stretching throughout the day. Rule of thumb is to stretch every 30 minutes for 2 minutes or every hour for 5 minutes.
- Use a stretch software program, such as RSI Guard. www.rsiguard.com

You can use Microsoft Outlook and set a reminder alert for stretching. Soon, stretching will become a good habit and your body will crave it.

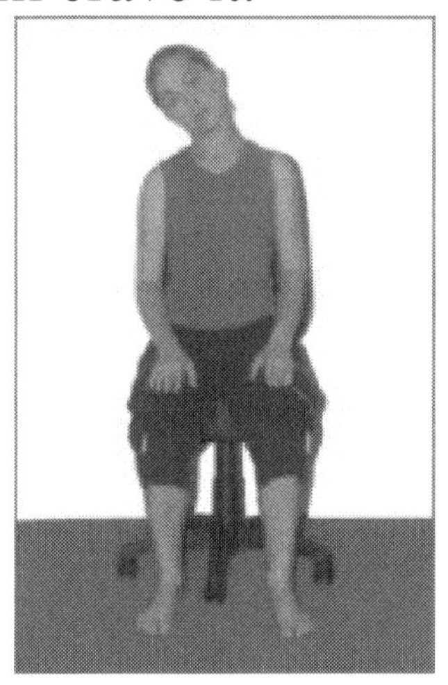

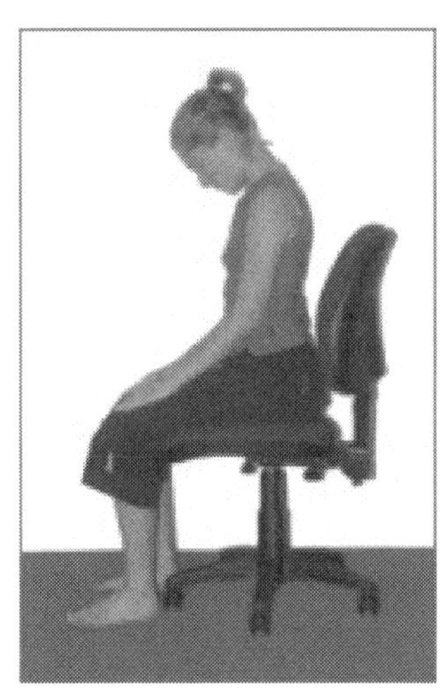

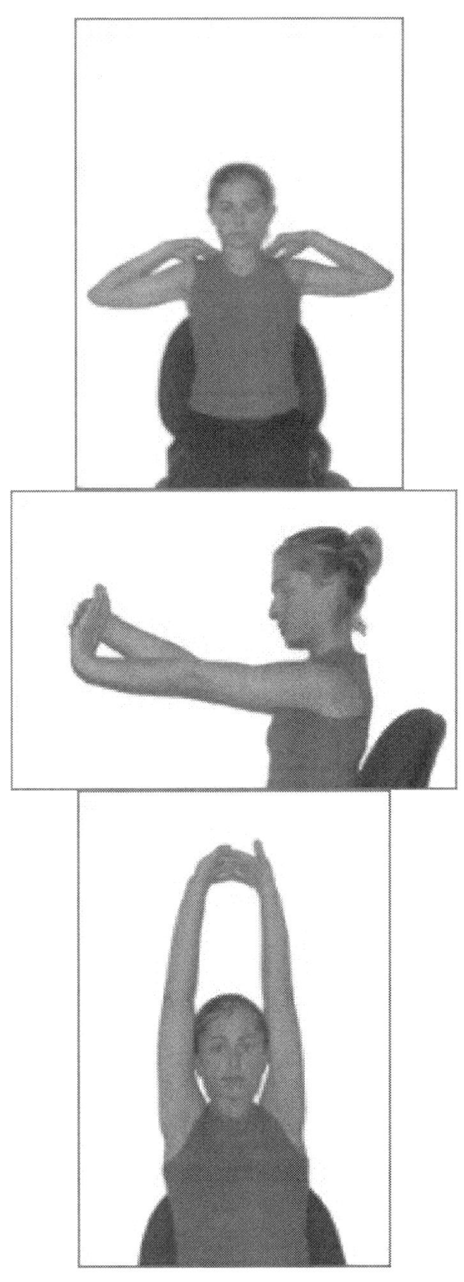

Remember

- We must learn to use our bodies correctly while working and living.
- It will take work to learn new habits. It always does.
- Be patient and soon without thinking, your movements will be done naturally and correctly.
- Always take care of yourself.

Chapter 6

Keyboarding Correctly

Let's go back a few years…Remember typewriters? If not, shame on you young person for already having to read this book! If you do remember, think back on how you typed. Did you rest your wrists? Were there gel wrist rests? Were you comfortable typing and slouching at the same time? Think back and try to remember.

Now think about today where we use computer keyboards. Are the keys laid out differently than on a typewriter? Do we type faster than we did 20 or 30 years ago? Was there a high incidence of Carpal Tunnel Syndrome (CTS)? Guess what? The answer to all of the questions is NO!

Typing on a typewriter required a little work and more motion of the arms. The keys were a bit tougher to press, so we actively typed. Now, because computer keyboards' keys are designed as *easy touch or soft touch*, little effort is required to use them. Unfortunately, this *little effort required* has resulted in sloppy posture and lazy habits. And, of course, injuries.

So, why are there so many problems today? One main reason is all the *lazy typing* out there! Many like to type while resting their wrists on their desk. I call this *static movement or a sure way to cause an injury*. When typing, we need more *active movement*.

As a machine for motion, the human body is made up of many bones, joints and muscles. Until recently, we had to be more active to survive. Getting from place to place, and our work and chores, demanded constant physical activity. A consequence of many tasks being automated is lack of movement. We can now work and play without moving much more than our finger tips. And, because the body was not designed for this inactivity, there is that reduction in blood flow and oxygen to the muscles which I talked about in Chapter 4.

The new buzzword in injuries is Carpal Tunnel Syndrome What is it? Well, everyone has carpal tunnel. It is the anatomical position on the wrist where all the nerves come together and pass through a tunnel. Carpel Tunnel Syndrome is when frequent pressure on this area compresses the nerves and causes damage, sometimes permanent. How do you know you might have it? Your fingers go numb, especially at night, or you pick up something and it flies out of your hand.

Before

After

How do you avoid Carpel Tunnel Syndrome?

Do not rest your wrists or forearms while typing. The soft wrist rests that are out there are called *wrist rests* for a reason. That is, they are for resting your wrists between typing, NOT while typing. By resting your wrists on the wrist rests while typing, you are making the smaller muscles in the fingers and forearms work harder and putting pressure on the nerves in your wrist. In turn, this could result in either tendonitis or carpal tunnel syndrome. To help prevent either of these injuries, develop the following good habits.

Take a rest from your wrist rest…

A wrist rest can alleviate contact stress from hard or sharp surfaces while working at the computer. However, you should not plant your wrist on it while using the keyboard or mouse. Continuous resting places pressure on the very spot you are trying to protect. Use the wrist rest only for pauses or breaks from keying. Let your fingers float over the keys like a pianist does while performing.

You'll perform better too.

Good Habits for Correct Keyboarding

1. Remove the wrist rest and don't rest the wrists when typing. Remember, it may take time to get used to typing without the wrist rests.
2. When not typing, rest the hands in your lap.
3. Place your keyboard at the edge of the desk or the keyboard tray.
4. Prop the feet up on the keyboard (like a typewriter), without the wrist rest.
5. Move and float your hands across the keys like you are playing the piano.
6. Type like it's an old typewriter and the keys need to be pushed a bit harder.
7. Only use the gel wrist rest when you're tired and need a break.

Chapter 7

Mousing 101

Like with keyboarding, resting the wrist when using the mouse causes the same pressure on the part of the wrist with the nerves. And, as with keyboarding, this pressure eventually compresses the nerves and causes damage. So, how does one use the mouse correctly? Has anyone ever been taught to use it? NO!

Incorrect Ways...

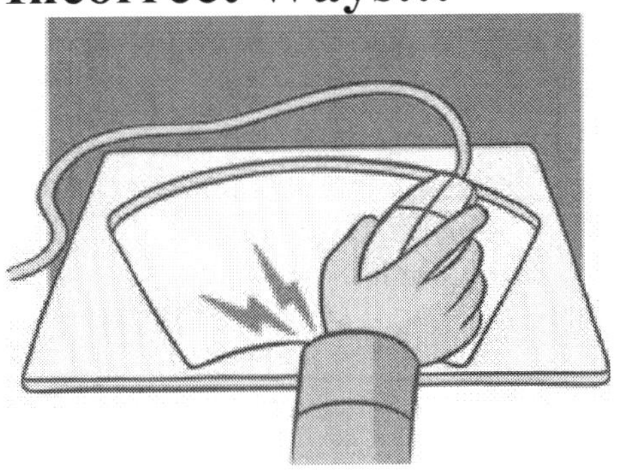

A flick of the wrist

Moving your mouse with a back-and-forth wrist movement, often known as "windshield wiping" increases risk of pain and injury to that area. Bending the wrist up, down, or to the side while mousing can place strain on the wrist nerves and tendons and cause inflammation and nerve entrapment. Place your whole hand on top of the mouse and use whole arm motions when operating a mouse and avoid doing the twist with your wrist.

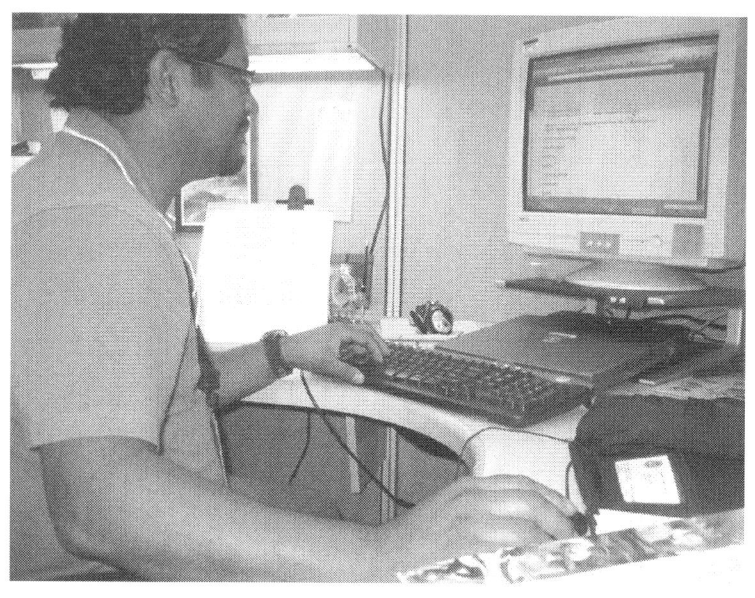

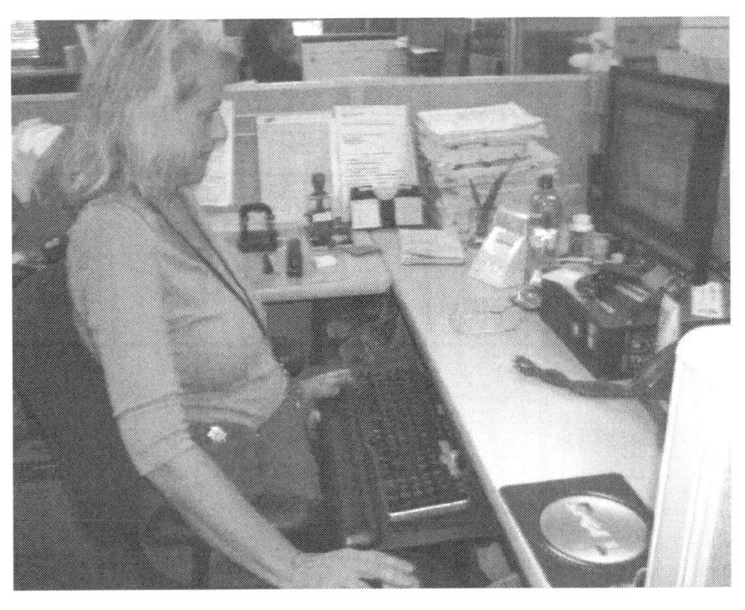

Tips on How to Mouse Correctly

1. Sit back in your chair, back straight and feet flat on the floor.
2. Remove the gel wrist rest if you are using one.
3. Move the mouse to the edge of your desk or tray.
4. Relax your arms and then lift your mousing hand up, bend at the elbow, until your hand is just above the mouse. Your mouse should be positioned somewhere around this position. If your mouse is in the correct position, you should not need to stretch forward or sideways to operate it.

5. Place the middle of the palm
   on the top mouse. Do not rest
   the lower part of the palm (the
   wrist) on the desktop or tray
   and gently grip the mouse.
   The weight of the arm should
   be in the middle of your palm.
6. Drape the fingers so they relax
   over the buttons. The finger
   tips may go over the end a bit.
7. To move the mouse, move the
   whole arm by using the larger
   muscle groups and not the tiny
   muscles of the hand and
   forearm.
8. Clicks are done gently with
   the middle knuckles, not
   the tip of the finger.
   If the mouse is covered by
   your palm, it is too small
   for your hand. Therefore
   you should purchase a
   larger or ergonomic
   mouse.

9. When purchasing a mouse,
    make sure it fits your hand, is
    as flat as possible, and that it
    encourages arm movement
    rather than wrist movement.
10. Remember though, there is
    really no such thing as the
    perfect mouse. All you can
    do is look for the mouse that
    best fits your hand and allows
    you to keep your wrist in a
    neutral position. And, if you
    use the mouse a lot, take
    frequent breaks to relieve the
    pressure on your wrist's
    nerves.

Incorrect

Correct

Incorrect

Correct

Chapter 8

A Good Workstation Set-Up

What can you do to your work environment to eliminate or reduce excessive reaching? Ask yourself, do you really need to stack the objects that high? Should you use a step stool? How do you have the objects situated? Heaviest at waist level, lightest on top and, those items not routinely moved down low.

Tips for Setting up an Ergonomically Healthy Workstation

Computer Screen

1. Clean your viewing screen
2. Adjust brightness and contrast
3. Avoid twisting by placing the monitor with the top of the viewing screen at eye level, about 20-26 inches directly in front of you
4. Position monitor to reduce glare from any windows or direct lighting

Chair

1. Ensure the height of backrest supports the natural inward curve of your lower back and the angle of the hip to torso is at 90 degrees or more
2. Ensure the height of the chair allows you to rest your feet flat on the floor and ensure your knees and hips are at least 90 degrees, or use a footrest
3. Ensure there is a 2-3 inch gap between the edge of the seat and the back of the knee
4. Ensure that the arm rests are adjusted so you can rest your arms at your sides and relax your shoulders when using the keyboard or mouse—or better yet remove the arm rests!

Desk

1. The working height of your desk should be at your elbow
2. The area under your desk should be clean so you can stretch your legs
3. Frequently used objects should be placed within arms reach to avoid over stretching
4. Document holders should be used to avoid excessive neck flexion and rotation
5. Keyboard should be close to you to avoid the need for reaching and its height adjusted so your shoulders can relax and your arms can rest at your sides

Lighting

Implement the following changes to reduce glare and avoid eyestrain, blurred vision, and other ailments related to your vision

1. Close drapes or blinds
2. Use low watt lights or dim one bulb
3. Adjust light source so that it is not direct on your screen or eyes
4. Paint your walls a medium or dark color and avoid reflective finishes
5. Use a glare screen or simply place a large manila envelope overhanging on top of your screen

Chapter 9

Equipment

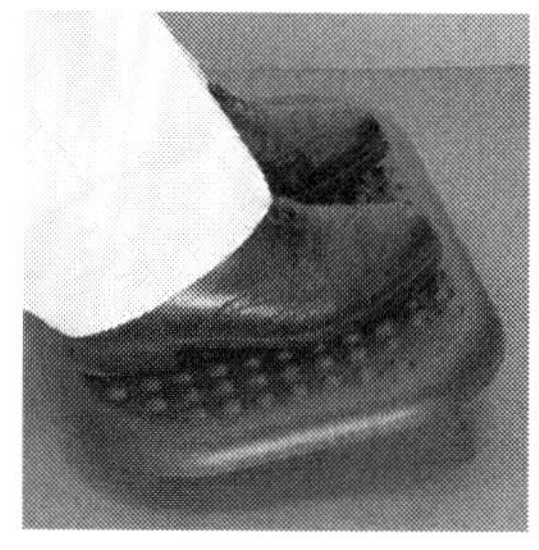 

Footrest   Roller Mouse

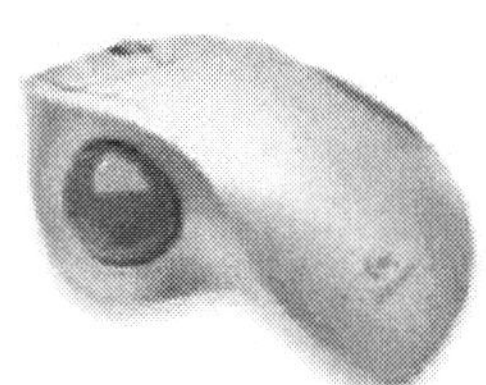 

Thumb Trackball   Marble

Ergonomic Optical Mouse

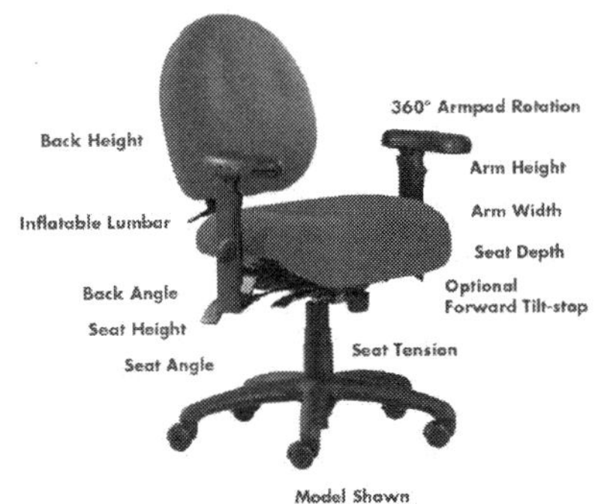

Ergonomic Chair

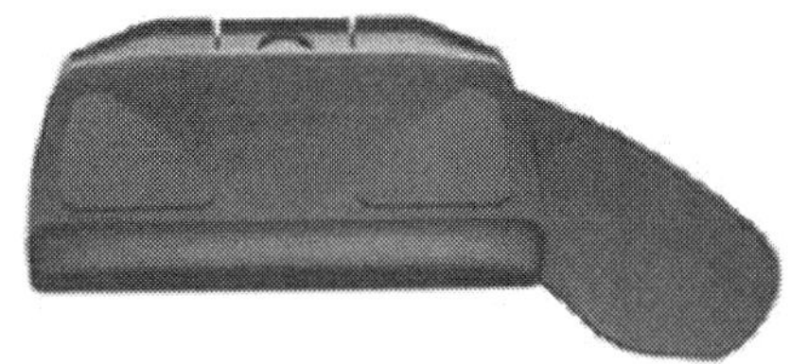

Articulating Keyboard/Mouse Tray

Ergonomic Keyboard

Mouse Bridge

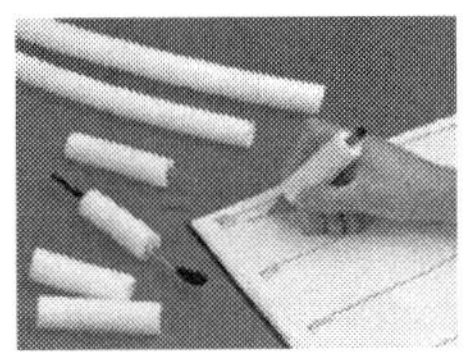

Foam Grips

Chapter 10

Evaluation Checklist

Work Posture

❏ Head and neck are upright or in line with the torso—not bent down or back

❏ Head, neck and body face forward —not twisted

❏ Body is perpendicular to the floor —may lean back into backrest but not forward

❏ Shoulders and upper arms are in line with the torso, perpendicular to the floor, and relaxed

❏ Upper arms and elbows are close to the body—not extended outward

❏ Forearms, wrists, and hands are straight and in line

❏ Wrists and hands are straight—not bent up, down, or sideways

❏ Thighs are parallel to the floor and the lower legs are roughly perpendicular to floor

❏ Feet rest flat on the floor or are supported by a stable footrest

❏ Alternate computer tasks and other activities or take short breaks to reduce fatigue

Chair

❏ Backrest supports the lower back—lumbar area

❏ Seat pan width and depth accommodate the user—seat pan not too big or small

❏ Seat pan does not press against the back of the knees and lower legs —seat pan not too long

❏ Seat pan is cushioned and rounded with a "waterfall" front—no sharp edge

❏ Armrests, if used, support the forearms and do not restrict movement

Keyboard and Mouse

❏ The keyboard platform is stable and large enough to hold a keyboard and a mouse

❏ The mouse is next to the keyboard so it can be operated without reaching

❏ The mouse is easy to activate and fits the hand comfortably

❏ Wrists and hands do not rest on sharp or hard edges

Monitor

❏ The top of the screen is at or below eye level so that it can be read without bending the neck

❏ Those who wear bifocal or trifocal lenses can read the screen without bending the neck

❏ The monitor distance allows one to read the screen without leaning forward or backward

❏ The monitor is directly in front of the user

❏Glare from windows or other light sources does not interfere with text or images on the screen

Desks or Other Work Surfaces

❏ There is enough space between the top of the user's thighs and the work surface or keyboard platform so that the thighs aren't trapped

❏ There is enough space under the work surface for the legs and feet so that the user can get close enough to the keyboard to type comfortably

Accessories

❏ The document holder is stable and large enough to hold documents

❏ The document holder is about the same height and distance from the user as the monitor screen

❏ Palm rests are padded and free of sharp or square edges

❏ Palm rests allow the forearms, wrists, and hands to remain in a straight line

❏ A telephone can be used with the head upright—not bent—and the shoulders relaxed

Chapter 11

Final Thoughts

An effective ergonomics program can result in healthier, injury-free employees, lower workers' comp costs, lower turnover, reduced overtime, and less need to hire new workers to replace those who have been injured. It may take time to re-learn these new postures and habits but, the long-term benefits will far outweigh the initial discomfort you may feel as your body readjusts to its correct posture.

Thanks and go out and have good postures!!

References:

www.stretchnow.com

www.clipart.com

www.cornell.com

www.arcergo.com

www.healthyback.com

www.ergomike.com

www.lifesavercprnow.com

www.oneworkplace.com

www.rsiguard.com

For more information, please
Contact ergochic@yahoo.com

Made in the USA
Monee, IL
07 July 2026